FORT GEORGE

Text by Iain MacIvor

Designed by
HMSO Graphic Design, Edinburgh

Principal photography by David Henrie

Photographs on pages 3, 5 and 10
reproduced by Gracious Permission of
Her Majesty The Queen.

Grateful thanks also to the following for
permission to reproduce photographs:
Argyll and Bute District Council (page 9)
The British Library (page 24)
Flying Cameras, Aviemore (page 8)
The National Library of Scotland (pages 4, 5,
    6, 8 and 18)
The Regimental Museum of the Queen's
    Own Highlanders (pages 9, 10 and 11)
The Viscount Gage (page 6)

Historic Buildings and Monuments
Scottish Development Department

Edinburgh
Her Majesty's Stationery Office

INTRODUCTION

*'The most considerable fortress and best
situated in Great Britain'*

Lt Col James Wolfe 1748

Fort George, one of the outstanding artillery fortifications in Europe, was begun by the government soon after the 1745-6 Jacobite rising to hinder any more armed threats to Hanoverian law and order. When building ended in 1769 the Highlands were peaceful, but the fort has continued in use ever since as a barracks.

The fort was planned as an impregnable base for George II's army, after the weakness of General Wade's small forts in the Highlands had been exposed during the rebellion. The new stronghold was designed to the highest standards of artillery fortification. Within the sophisticated defences, William Skinner (later appointed governor of the fort as a reward for his services) designed comprehensive ranges of buildings on a monumental scale to accommodate the governor and other officers of the fortress, the artillery detachment, and the garrison of 1600 infantry. The buildings included a powder magazine, ordnance and provision stores, a bakehouse, brewhouse and chapel. The building contract was held by John Adam, occasioning frequent visits by his famous brothers, Robert and James.

Although the Jacobite threat had evaporated by the completion date, the fort continued in use, and very little alteration or addition was made to either the defences or internal buildings, even after the fortifications were clearly no longer needed. After 1881 it was used exclusively as the depot of the Seaforth Highlanders. The superlative distinction of Fort George today is that there survive intact not only the bastioned defences with all their outworks, but also the whole of the interior ranges, which in their own right are an outstanding example of military architecture.

The first part of this guide-book outlines the story of the Highland garrisons before Culloden, gives an account of the beginnings and the building of the fort, and concludes with a brief history up to the present day. The second part of the guide is a descriptive tour.

Below left: A soldier of the 42nd Regiment of Foot (later known as The Black Watch), painted by David Morier about 1750. Morier, a native of Switzerland, worked under the patronage of the Duke of Cumberland and recorded all the regiments in the Hanoverian army.

Below: The armorials of the principal gate. These are quarterly, with England impaling Scotland in the first quarter, France in the second, Ireland in the third and Hanover in the fourth.

A Plan of a New Fort design'd for *INVERNESS*, Done exactly upon the Old Lines of _____ *OLIVERS FORT*, with the additional Outworks of *COVER'D-WAY-LUNETTES*, & *GLASSIS*, all which are more fully explained in the particular *PLAN's* *SECTIONS*. _____

EXPLANATION

Protector Cromwell's fort at Inverness, begun by Major-General Deane in 1652 and finished in 1657. The fort was slighted in 1661 but proposals (shown here) were made by the Board of Ordnance in 1746 to convert it into a garrison fortress for the Hanoverian army of King George II.

Ruthven Barracks, in Badenoch, built between 1719 and 1721 for the Hanoverian government by Sir Patrick Strachan of Glenkindie to accommodate up to 120 'redcoats'. After heroically withstanding a Jacobite force in the earliest days of the '45 rebellion, the garrison surrendered in 1746, shortly before Culloden. After their defeat, the leading Jacobites retired to Ruthven Barracks before going their separate ways.

THE STORY OF THE FORT

'A large sum of money spended in building'

James Boswell 1773

Highland garrisons before Culloden

The Highlands had given concern to the central government of Scotland since the middle ages. The ancient way of life of the inhabitants always caused anxiety to neighbours, and often created more general alarm. After 1651, Oliver Cromwell's military occupation added disaffection to normal unruliness. The English built a large artillery fort at Inverness and a smaller one at Inverlochy, at the bottom end of the Great Glen. Nothing like these forts had been seen in the Highlands before.

Cromwell's forts were slighted after the restoration of Charles II, but following the 1688 revolution, when William III's authority had to be enforced in the Highlands by his army, the fort at Inverlochy was rebuilt and named Fort William after him; the fort at Inverness remained in ruins, while the ancient castle in the town was strengthened.

The welcome extended to George I by his new subjects was tempered by the 1715 Jacobite rising. The Jacobites (from the Latin *Jacobus* meaning James) supporting the exiled James VII were disarmed and in 1717 four infantry barracks were built to augment the forts at Inverness Castle and Fort William. The largest was at the south end of Loch Ness, near where Fort Augustus was later built. A smaller barracks was at Ruthven, near Kingussie in Inverness-shire. The other two were at Bernera in Glenelg, on the western seaboard facing across to Skye, and Inversnaid in Stirlingshire, in the shadow of Ben Lomond.

Despite government action, lawlessness and Jacobite disaffection continued. In 1724 Major-General Wade was ordered to look into the situation and, as a result, the first military roads were constructed. Fort Augustus was built to replace the nearby barracks, and new works were raised round Inverness Castle which became the first Fort George. Wade saw his forts, with Fort William, as a chain linked by its military road to secure the strategically important Great Glen.

The Highlanders were not impressed. The Great Glen forts were ignored in the first part of the 1745 rising and did not impede its progress. Early in 1746 Prince Charles Edward

PLAN
of
FORT GEORGE
at INVERNESS
Shewing its present Condition
1746
EXPLANATION

Fort George, Inverness, as slighted by the Jacobites before Culloden. The buildings are burnt out and great piles of rubble mark the positions of the mines sprung by the Jacobites after the surrender. The massive rectangular tower of the ancient castle stands to the right of the barrack square. All traces of the ruins were removed when the present buildings, designed as a County Hall and prison, were built in the nineteenth century.

Far left: The Battle of Culloden, 16 April 1746, painted by Thomas Sandby for the Hanoverian government.

Above: The first Fort George, at Inverness Castle, in 1744 before the Jacobites destroyed it in the days leading up to Culloden.

Stuart's commanders decided to reduce the forts to allow more freedom of manoeuvre in the Highland campaign which was contemplated after the withdrawal from Derby. Inverness fell easily. At Fort Augustus a shell detonated the powder magazine and the fort surrendered. Fort William put up a more creditable defence, due more to the spirit of the garrison than to the advantages given by the fortifications. The siege there was raised a fortnight before Culloden.

That battle on 16 April 1746 ended Jacobite hopes of further resistance. But the ruins of the two forts were a humiliating and cautionary spectacle for the victorious Hanoverian army. All the measures that had been taken so far had been ineffective. The martial prowess of the Highlanders would not be underestimated next time by King George II's government.

King George II at the battle of Dettingen, 1743.

Above: An Adam fireplace in the governor's house.

A craftsman — Johne Swinton, carpenter and joiner, chalks his name on a joist in the top floor of the governor's house in 1767.

A detailed plan of the elaborate outworks on the landward, or eastern front.

William Skinner (1700-80), who designed Fort George, and his daughter, Susannah, later Viscountess Gage. From a portrait by Thomas Beach at Firle Place, Sussex.

William Skinner's design for Fort George, Ardersier. The pink rectangle to the left denotes the only standing structure on 'this barren, sandy point' in 1747 — a fisherman's hut on the earl of Cawdor's estate.

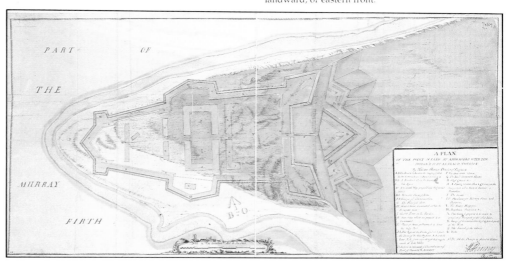

Fort George, Ardersier

Ambitious plans were drawn up for a new Fort Augustus but were not carried out and in 1748 Wade's fort was rebuilt with only minor improvements. A design for the reconstruction of Cromwell's fort at Inverness was made in 1746 by an Irish engineer, and in the following year a second design was made by William Skinner, newly-appointed as military engineer for North Britain. Skinner's design was accepted. The building contract was let to William Adam. Work was about to begin when the Burgh Council of Inverness claimed compensation for loss of use of the harbour close to the fort. The Board dropped the scheme and Skinner hastily looked for another site. In late 1747 he conceived a plan for a new works on a barren spit of land jutting into the Moray Firth at Ardersier, 14.5 km east of Inverness.

The new site proved much better. The Ardersier promontory was spacious and its isolation made it much stronger. The site was overlooked by high ground 1.6 km to the east, but in the eighteenth century such a range was just beyond the effective capability of guns and howitzers.

The shape of the promontory suggested a design with its landward defences concentrated on one front, the east. Sea defence would not be neglected but it could be limited to the encircling rampart. Thus resources could be concentrated on defence in depth of the east front. Here the main rampart would form the innermost line of defence. Beyond, a complex arrangement of outworks would help keep a besieger at a distance and delay his advance, as well as provide an assembly area for a counter-attack.

The internal buildings were to hold two infantry battalions (1600 men) and an artillery unit. Under siege, the garrison would retire to vaulted barrack-rooms, called casemates, built under the rampart, where they would be safe from the high-angle fire of heavy mortars. The entire cost was estimated at £92,673 19s 1d. The actual bill came to more than double that; but Skinner's assistant who worked out the quantities and prices might reasonably plead that he was hard-pressed for time, for work began in 1748.

Building the fort raised problems. There was plenty of local unskilled labour, and Skinner could also call on the military for earthmoving, but there were few local tradesmen. The main contractors and many of their men came from the Lowlands. (Although William Adam died in 1748, his contract remained with the family firm, headed by his eldest son, John.) Almost all the building materials had to be brought in by sea. The fort was the biggest construction job ever undertaken in the Highlands, not to be exceeded until the digging of the Caledonian Canal in the next century.

The royal cipher of King George III and the date cast into a rainwater hopper upon one of the barrack blocks.

Even under normal conditions it would have been an exacting task to erect works covering 17 hectares (42 acres) and containing enough buildings for a small town. The fort, however, was not built under normal conditions. The site had to be secured immediately against attack and thereafter kept in a state of readiness. Operations began on the east front, while a pier was built south of the fort to land materials. In 1750 a temporary palisade was set up round the rest of the site, which could then be defended after a fashion. At that time, when the most extensive earthmoving was being undertaken, more than 1000 soldiers and labourers were probably employed.

Graffiti scratched on stonework during the building operations.

Next the defences were reinforced by the ravelin, a large artillery work, ready for occupation in 1753. This acted as a redoubt while the main rampart was being built. Eight guns were placed there, and eight more put on the great mounds of earth which had been raised for the bastions.

By now the internal buildings were beginning to rise and some accommodation was ready in 1757. At the end of that year the defences were well advanced but were untidy and lacking finishing touches. In 1760 the fort received its main armament. The last building inside the fort, the chapel, was begun in 1763 and the final undertaking was the replacement of the temporary structures over the ditches by permanent bridges. By 1769 the work was nearly finished. Although we do not know the original target date for completion, it is clear that progress had fallen behind schedule. The final cost of well over £200000 was more than Scotland's annual Gross National Product for 1750.

Corgarff Castle, a medieval tower house of the Forbes family, requisitioned by the military authorities in 1748 and converted into a soldiers' barrack to aid the policing of this remote and lawless region.

Far right: General Skinner's plans for the conversion of Corgarff Castle into a barracks for a company of soldiers (about 60 men), to be outposted from Fort George.

Fort George was not the only work inspired by the '45. The system of military roads was greatly enlarged — by 1767 there were over 1600 km of them. The road from Blairgowrie to Fort George was built in 1749-54. In 1748 existing tower houses on its route at Braemar and Corgarff were converted into small barracks, from which active patrols of redcoats could police the remote glens.

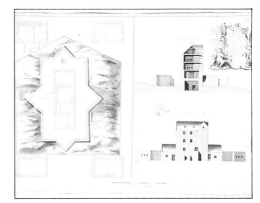

'AD 1754 Five companies the 33rd Regiment Right Honle Lord Chas Hay Colonel made the road from here to the Spey': an inscription at the Well of the Lecht near Tomintoul, north of Corgarff Castle, beside the military road from Blairgowrie to Fort George. The road at the Well of the Lecht is still in use as the A939.

Far right: The military road from Blairgowrie to Fort George, south of Corgarff Castle, built 1749-54.

Invercauld Bridge, near Braemar, one of the finest bridges on the Blairgowrie-Fort George military road and now in state care.

Later history

While Fort George was being built, Jacobite disaffection became a romantic notion. Rapid social and economic change aided the political and military measures taken after Culloden to pacify the Highlands. By 1770 the local population regarded the new fort as a costly mistake — not quite a fair criticism, for in 1748 no-one could have guessed that the Highland problem would so rapidly cease to be a military one. Various line regiments succeeded each other as the garrison. When Samuel Johnson and James Boswell called in 1773, the 37th Foot was stationed there.

In 1778 the 73rd Highland Regiment of Foot — one of the ancestors of the Royal Highland Fusiliers — embarked at Fort George after being raised in Elgin. Thus began a new use for the station. Most of the numerous Highland regiments which were embodied in the later part of the eighteenth century spent a few weeks or months there while being either mustered, equipped, inspected, embarked, disembarked or, eventually, disbanded. One such casual encounter later flowered into a more lasting union. In July 1793 the newly-formed 78th Highlanders paraded at the fort. The 78th returned at rare intervals in the nineteenth century until, in 1881, Fort George became the depot of the Seaforth Highlanders, then formed by the amalgamation of the 72nd and 78th.

The fort had entertained more enduring occupants besides its visitors in transit (who were not confined to Highland units). In 1795 the permanent garrison consisted of a company of 'Invalids' — men unfit for active service but capable of garrison duty — and an artillery unit. Then, and for many years after, the guns on the ramparts were kept in readiness for action that never came. It was perhaps just as well. By the end of the Napoleonic Wars military men were doubtful of the effectiveness of the fort should it be put to the test. Improved artillery and the recent invention of the shrapnel shell meant that the east front was now uncomfortably dominated by the high ground beyond it. The place was no longer a first-rate stronghold.

After Waterloo in 1815, Fort George apparently was considered as a location for the imprisonment of Napoleon but lost out to St Helena. No doubt to the London-based authorities Fort George and an island in the Mid Atlantic were equally remote! Certainly, the fort's continued use as a barracks was seriously in doubt now that peace had come.

Recruiting Highlanders at Campbeltown Fair, Argyll, by Archibald Mackinnon.

In 1817 an order to dismantle all the Highland forts was given then countermanded. In 1835 it was proposed to convert Fort George into a prison (it had previously served as a place of confinement for political prisoners from Ireland) but the idea came to nothing. Fort George was reprieved during the French invasion scare of the 1850s and around 1860 a powerful coastal-defence battery was built on its sea-facing ramparts. The new guns became the fort's main armament. The once formidable east front might still be adequate to fend off an enemy by land, provided he were not equipped with a full siege train. The century-old buildings of the fort fell below contemporary standards but were capable of improvement.

Life and death at Fort George in the eighteenth century.

Fort George from the Moray
Firth.

A contemporary and
humorous view of the war
against Napoleon, stressing
the importance of the
Highland regiments in the
heady days of Empire. Many
of those who fought and
died overseas began their
army life at Fort George.

Far right: A soldier of the
Invalids Regiment, men
unfit for active service but
capable of garrison duty —
the 'Dad's Army' of the
eighteenth century. Painted
by David Morier.

Nothing though could reprieve Fort Augustus and Fort William. Unwanted and neglected, they kept up a shaky military appearance until the Crimean War and were sold soon afterwards. Fort Augustus eventually took on a new prosperous existence as a Benedictine abbey; Fort William, less auspiciously, became the locomotive depot of the North British Railway. Fort George was then the only active reminder of the widespread eighteenth-century military presence in the Highlands. The barracks of 1717 had long been derelict, though the little 1748 barracks at Corgarff and Braemar castles prolonged their working lives well into the nineteenth century as bases for soldiers helping the excisemen against smuggling and illicit distilling. (The garrisons were detached from the Invalids stationed at Fort George.) The military roads had been taken over by the Commissioners of Roads and Bridges in 1814: most were improved, a few were abandoned.

The Victorian coastal battery at Fort George did not keep its value for long. Within a decade its smooth-bore muzzle-loaded guns were outclassed by revolutionary built-up rifled ordnance. The performance of the new weapons also finally made such a bastioned fortification as Fort George quite indefensible.

Though some of the guns and mortars remained until 1881, they were by then decorative rather than useful.

The 1881 reorganisation of the army with territorial depots infused new life into Fort George, which remained the Seaforth Highlanders' depot until 1961 when the regiment was amalgamated with the Cameron Highlanders to form the Queen's Own Highlanders. When the latter marched out in 1964, the connection with the Seaforths was not severed for their Regimental Association remains in the fort together with the museum of the Queen's Own Highlanders.

The Ministry of Public Building and Works began to look after Fort George on behalf of the Ministry of Defence in 1964, and it was first opened to the public as an Ancient Monument in that year. In 1967 it was once more occupied by regular soldiers, the Royal Highland Fusiliers, who found that the stately Georgian fortress was still able to satisfy their needs. Today Fort George's future as an army barracks is assured following a comprehensive reorganisation of the accommodation by the Ministry of Defence, the only Ancient Monument in Scotland still functioning as originally intended.

A heavy traversing gun, part of the Victorian coastal defence battery, on Duke of Cumberland's Bastion in the 1870s shortly before the fort's armament was recalled to London in 1881.

Officers of the Ross-shire Rifles pose outside the officers' mess, formerly the governor's house, in the 1870s.

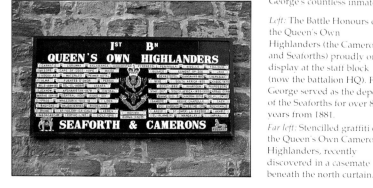

Above: Graffiti scratched onto the outworks by one of Fort George's countless inmates.

Left: The Battle Honours of the Queen's Own Highlanders (the Camerons and Seaforths) proudly on display at the staff block (now the battalion HQ). Fort George served as the depot of the Seaforths for over 80 years from 1881.

Far left: Stencilled graffiti of the Queen's Own Cameron Highlanders, recently discovered in a casemate beneath the north curtain.

FORT GEORGE

1 Visitors' car park

2 Ravelin guardhouse and visitor centre

3 Principal bridge

4 Principal gate and guardrooms

5 Prince of Wales's bastion

6 South casemated curtain and sallyport

7 Prince William Henry's bastion

8 Prince Frederick William's demi-bastion

9 Point battery

10 Duke of Marlborough's demi-bastion

11 Prince Henry Frederick's bastion

12 North casemated curtain and sallyport

13 Dog cemetery

14 Duke of Cumberland's bastion

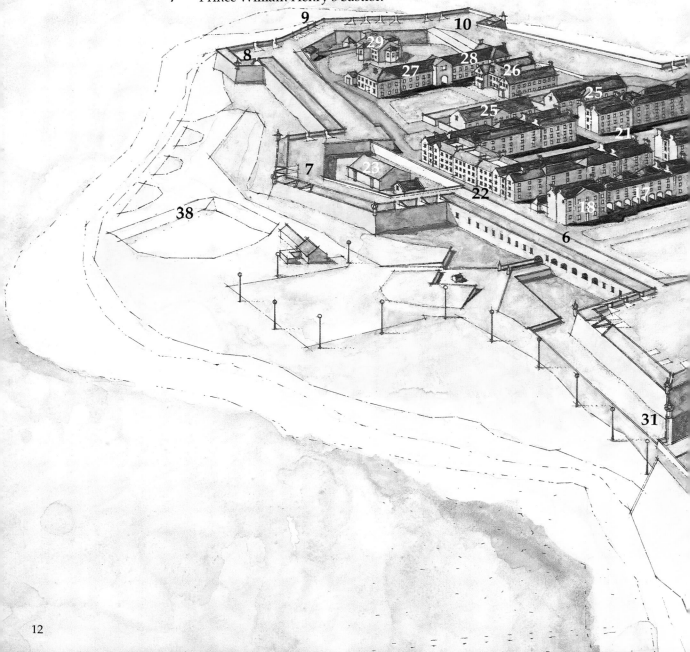

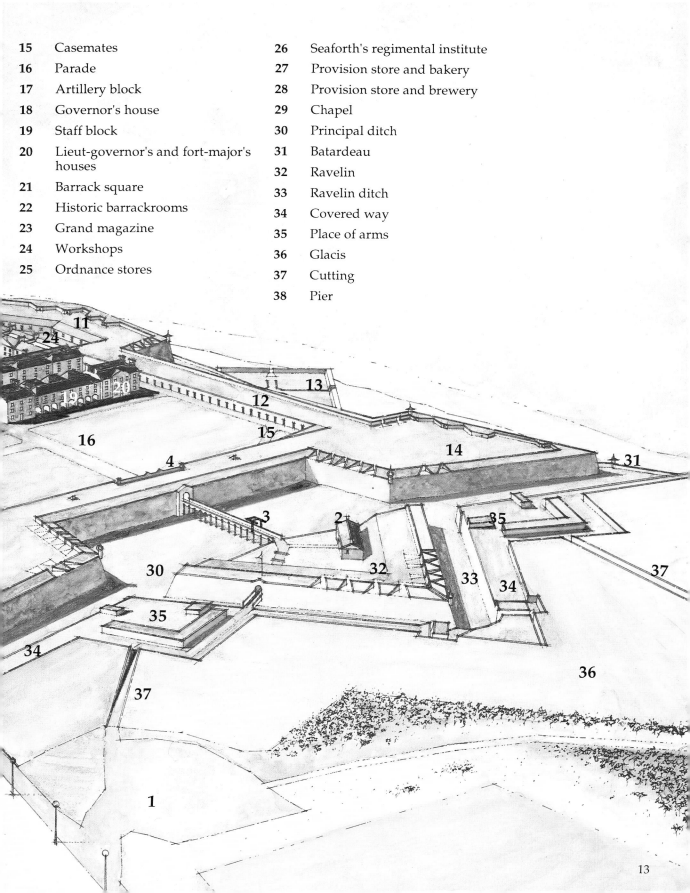

A TOUR OF THE FORT

*'Impregnable against any force
sent against it'*

Lord Ligonier 1759

The principal bridge and gate

The main body of the fort is approached over the ditch by a bridge (1765-6) at the centre of the east curtain. The third span from the ravelin was a drawbridge operated by upper counterpoise beams (reinstated, following the original plans, in 1980). The innermost span, against the principal gate, was also a drawbridge which could be raised to cover the gate. Both drawbridges survived until about 1900 by which time the whole bridge was in a very decayed state: for some time the enlarged south sallyport had been used as the chief entrance and the original approach was neglected.

The design for the principal gate was made originally by Skinner as part of his abortive project to rebuild Cromwell's fort at Inverness, and was carried out without change at Ardersier in 1753-6. Contrasting yellow and red sandstone emphasises pairs of Doric pilasters, supporting a heavy pediment bearing the royal arms. The gate leads into a **tunnel,** vaulted in brick, beneath the rampart; the tunnel still has its original massive double-leaved, studded and barred doors hung in 1766 (for the previous decade the entrance had only temporary barriers). The tunnel opens out into an arcaded **vestibule.** At the south-east side of the vestibule a door leads to a stair communicating with the ditch below the principal gate.

The guardrooms

On either side of the vestibule behind the principal gate are two vaulted chambers housing the main guard of the fort. The smaller guardroom, on the north side, was for officers: the larger guardroom on the south was for non-commissioned officers and men. Behind the officers' guardroom is the prison — known in the eighteenth and early nineteenth centuries as the 'Black Hole'. It was abandoned when new cells were incorporated into the north provision store in the nineteenth century (see page 21), but not before David Abernethy, serving 60 days for being drunk on guard, had carved his name and crime on one of the walls in 1831.

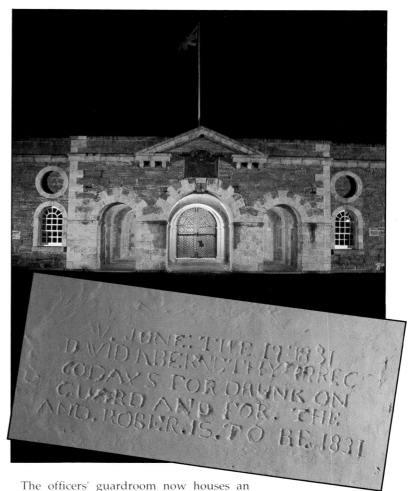

The principal gate floodlit.

Inset: David Abernethy's graffiti in the prison beside the principal gate.

The officers' guardroom now houses an **exhibition** highlighting important aspects of army life in the century following the building of the fort, told through the soldiers' own words and contemporary illustrations. The soldiers' guardroom has been recreated as a guardroom of the 1880s, when the fort was serving as the depot of the Seaforth Highlanders. When Fort George was built, the men slept on a communal wooden shelf-bed placed against the east wall. By 1880 this had been replaced by the metal turn-up beds there today.

Standing Orders in 1808 required the 'sentinels ... at the guardhouse door ... to take charge of all prisoners, turn out the guard to all field officers. Not to suffer people to wash at the pumps, nor to allow children or idle people to play about them or any dirty water to be emptied near them. He is to attend to the call of the sentry at the Gate and to warn the sergeant of the guard and to keep people from walking on the grass path excepting officers and their families'.

Top: Firepower: The armament on Duke of Cumberland's Bastion.

Middle: Firepower: The Armstrong Mk 1 rifled gun of 1865 mounted on the Victorian traversing platform at the point of Duke of Cumberland's Bastion.

Bottom: The south curtain with its sallyport.

The rampart

The main defence is the rampart forming a continuous line round the fort, made up of bastions and demi-bastions (half bastions) joined by lengths of curtain wall. It is reached by six ramps around the interior. The bastions and the ravelin were named after close relatives of George II. George, Prince of Wales (who succeeded to the throne in 1760) was his eldest grandson.

All bastions have a polygonal plan made up of two *faces* towards the field and two *flanks*. Their design gives a complete cover of defensive fire from the cannon embrasures and musketry firing-step at the parapet level of the flanks, along the adjoining lengths of curtain (called *scarps)* and across to the adjacent bastions. Behind the parapet is a broad level fighting platform, called the *terreplein,* providing ample space for the movement of men and for the construction of additional defences in time of siege. The outer angles of the bastions are capped by sentry-boxes from which the whole of the scarps might be observed. At the *salients,* or outward-pointing angles, of the east bastion the terreplein is raised for long-range batteries firing 'in barbette' over the parapets. Four heavy mortars, capable of firing bombs up to 2.4 km in front of the fort, were emplaced on the terreplein of the east rampart. They were subsequently removed, together with the rest of the fort's artillery, towards the close of the nineteenth century. The guns and mortars there now are not the original armament but they convey an impression of its former firepower.

Prince of Wales's Bastion survives as built. Apart from the four heavy guns of the barbette battery, there are embrasures for two more heavy guns firing out to sea from the south face, and for nine lighter pieces; five on the north flank covering the main ditch, two on the east face covering the ravelin ditch, and two on the west flank covering the south sallyport. The east face of this bastion gives a very good general view of the outworks on the east front and a **viewing point** identifies the various defensive elements.

The **south casemated curtain** between Prince of Wales's Bastion and Prince William Henry's Bastion, and the corresponding length of curtain of the north rampart, had casemated barrack-rooms for accommodation in times of siege (see page 17). In the middle of the curtain a **sallyport** leads out to a **place of arms** (1761-5), a mustering point for a sortie. The sallyport has been enlarged to form the modern main entry to the fort and the east end of the place of arms has been removed to improve the approach road.

In the middle of the south front is **Prince William Henry's Bastion,** named after George II's third grandson. The best view of the main powder store, the grand magazine, may be had from this bastion, which encloses it. From the east face of the bastion may be seen a pool of water, landlocked behind a shingle bank. To the east of the pool, and no longer visible, was the pier constructed to land building materials for the fort. To the west of the pool is the surviving later **pier,** used to bring ashore supplies for the garrison, to serve the civilian ferry across to Chanonry Point, and to embark and disembark many of the units which passed through the fort. Thus from the very beginning the south sallyport took a great deal of traffic. At first it also took civilians using the ferry, who had to go right through the fort between the south sallyport and the principal gate, most inconveniently for

travellers and soldiers alike. In about 1790 a new cutting was made through the *glacis* (counterscarp bank) of the east front for the travellers: the cutting was covered by the guns on the east flank of Prince William Henry's Bastion. Though it was not so intended, the new opening through the glacis provided a short cut to the fort itself from the east. The sallyport was subsequently widened and replaced the intentionally awkward approach through the east front as the main entry.

The west end of the fort is designed as two **demi-bastions,** named after George II's youngest grandson, **Frederick William,** and the **Duke of Marlborough,** on each side of the **Point Battery** commanding the channel between the fort and Chanonry Point. The battery had twenty artillery embrasures on the terreplein and two on the flanks of the demi-bastions. Embrasures on the north and south faces of the demi-bastions were soon blocked — possibly while building was still in progress. Below the terreplein the Point Battery had a small powder magazine, and casemates for four 32-pounder guns, installed in 1760. The casemates, completed in 1758, were one of Skinner's few modifications to his original design. They were subsequently blocked up.

About 1860 a coastal-defence battery was installed in the north and west fronts of the fort. The new gun emplacements have destroyed parts of the parapet and some of the sentry boxes, including those of the Point Battery, which held three of the new weapons. These weapons were set on wooden platforms which traversed on iron rails.

Three guns of the coastal battery were mounted on **Prince Henry Frederick's Bastion** (George II's fourth grandson), replacing four original embrasures. Beside the gun mountings are small expense magazines and shot and shell recesses built into and under the thickened parapet. The hollow centre of the bastion contains the workshop yard.

In the middle of the **north casemated curtain** an unaltered sallyport leads to the **north place of arms.** The sea soon washed part of this away and it was rebuilt as it exists now. It was later used by the Seaforth Highlanders as a cemetery for their pet dogs.

Half of the original barbette battery in **Duke of Cumberland's Bastion** (George II's brother) was removed when the Victorian emplacements were built; the rest was modified not long afterwards when three gun platforms were formed and the brick parapet

wall rebuilt to its present indented shape. A 64-pounder Armstrong Mark I rifled gun of 1865 (the sole survivor of its type) is now mounted on a replica carriage at the salient of the bastion.

Descending the north-east ramp from Duke of Cumberland's Bastion, the pair of accessible **casemates** nearby may be visited. Casemated barrack-rooms providing accommodation in times of siege were built under both the north and south curtains. Each curtain could hold about 700 men in 27 casemates, up to 40 men to a casemate. As built, each had a shuttered ventilating slit on either side of the door and a roundel above it. There were no openings through the far scarp wall and a fireplace was the only internal fixture. As the overriding need for security declined, the casemates were improved by increasing the size of the windows around the doors and by punching new apertures through the scarp wall. In the nineteenth century they were frequently used by militia units in preference to living under canvas on the heath outside the fort. They were used from the beginning for storage and that is the function they largely serve today.

Firepower: A heavy 13" iron mortar with its bombs emplaced on the east rampart.

The internal buildings

Skinner's buildings were planned symmetrically and generously surrounded by open space. Though some have been altered and added to, all survive in a remarkable state of preservation and make up a most outstanding architectural group. It is the survival of the buildings contemporary with the fortifications that gives the fort its unique quality.

The parade

The eastern part of the interior was the parade. From the beginning it has been a broad expanse of turf where officers and their families could take their exercise. It was, and still is, used for ceremonial parades. Normal drill has always been carried out on the barrack square.

The artillery and staff blocks

The artillery block (1762-6) and the staff block (1761-6) make up an imposing façade closing the west side of the parade. The building with pediment and portico at the south end of the artillery block was the governor's house, now the officers' mess. As an honour for his services William Skinner was appointed the first governor of the fort. As its first occupant, Skinner had the responsibility for decorating the governor's house. The fittings included two fireplaces by James Adam. The rest of the artillery block housed the detachment of gunners manning the armament of the fort: the men above the piazza, the officers in the north pavilion. The staff block contained quarters for staff and storekeepers with, at its north end, the elegant building which provided houses for the lieutenant-governor and the fort major. This pavilion now serves as the **Regimental Museum** of the Queen's Own Highlanders.

The barracks

The two 'piles' of barracks accommodated two infantry battalions. They were the first structures inside the fort to be begun in 1753. The north range was finished in 1761, the south range in 1764. (The dates 1757 and 1763 on the pediments of the central pavilions of the two ranges mark the completion of the pavilions, not the ranges as a whole.) The central and terminal pavilions in both ranges were for officers; the men occupied the remainder. Regular drill was carried out on the large **barrack square** between the two ranges.

Above: The artillery and staff blocks from across the parade.

Right: Major Andrew Coghlan's quarters, 1813.

Below: The Board of Ordnance design for the barracks.

The historic barrack-rooms

A stretch of corridor with three rooms off, in the south barrack range, is open to the public (the remainder is under army occupation). They have been reconstructed to show what living conditions might have been like in the century after the fort's completion.

Two are soldiers' barrack-rooms — one of 1780, the other of 1868 — illustrating the astonishing improvements in accommodation for the rank and file during that period. In 1780 Private John Anderson and his comrades of the 42nd Royal Highlanders slept two to a bed, eight to a room. There were no communal messing, toilet or recreational facilities. The men drew their daily rations from the provision stores and cooked for themselves. One in every hundred soldiers was allowed to 'marry on the strength'. Their wives, and any children, lived in and received half rations in exchange for doing domestic chores. Their only concession to privacy was a blanket drawn across their corner of the barrack-room. Life in barracks must have been tediously dull, the days punctuated with irregular drills and infrequent guard duties, and nothing but a crowded room to spend their idle hours in.

The contrast with Private George Moffat's barrack-room of 1868 could not be more striking. By this date married quarters had been acknowledged as a necessity; so, too, the requirement for communal messing, toilet, and recreational facilities. As a consequence, the amount of space per man was almost doubled and the atmosphere in the room greatly improved. There were now just five men to the room, sleeping in single beds, and they were encouraged to do anything but be idle and drunk.

The officer's room, set at the time of the Napoleonic Wars, in 1813, is noticeably more amenable than those for the rank and file. More spacious and lighter, with larger window panes (by standing in the barrack square one can readily distinguish accommodation reserved for officers by this one detail), it has other little flourishes such as window shutters, fine panelled doors and a mantlepiece. The room, though, is far from luxurious. The life of an officer, even a quite senior officer like Major Coghlan, who was Commanding Officer at the fort in 1813, was as uncertain as that of his men and his pay barely sufficient to keep him in the manner expected of him by his regiment. All he possessed had to be capable of being transported on campaign: hence the folding-bed, travelling chest and trunk.

Private George Moffat's barrack-room, 1868.

Private John Anderson's barrack-room, 1780.

The grand magazine

In the centre of Prince William Henry's Bastion was the main powder magazine. Quickly raised in 1757-9, it was given timber racking for 2500 barrels of gunpowder. The building has a complicated design, for it had to be robust enough to withstand a direct hit from a mortar bomb, and cool enough internally to keep the powder dry; hence the slated roof laid on massive brick vaults supported on square stone pillars, and the provision of wall vents and a raised timber floor. To reduce the risk of explosion, there were no ferrous fittings: all doors and vent shutters, even the rhones and downpipes, were either sheathed in or made from copper; and the raised floor was fixed with wooden dowels.

The Seafield Collection

On display in the grand magazine is an outstanding collection of arms and military equipment — the Seafield Collection, so called because it passed to the crown from the estate of the Dowager Countess of Seafield. Most of the collection dates from the time of the Napoleonic Wars, when Sir James Grant, chief of Clan Grant and Lord Lieutenant of Inverness-shire, was active in raising and equipping regiments from the lands under his influence. They included the Strathspey Fencible Regiment (raised in 1793), the 97th Regiment of Foot and the Inverness-shire Volunteers (raised in 1794) and the Inverness-shire Militia (raised in 1802).

The collection includes India-pattern

The crouching mass of the grand magazine, solidly built to withstand a direct hit from a mortar bomb.

Right: The stand of muskets and pikes from the Seafield Collection of arms and military equipment.

Far right: The grand magazine stacked high with replica (and empty!) powder barrels.

muskets with bayonets (the standard-issue gun from 1794); pikes issued to the Strathspey company of the Inverness-shire Volunteers as an economy measure at a time when muskets were in short supply; ammunition pouches (of 'stoutest blackened calf skin … to turn the severest rain'); knapsacks (of 'stout canvass, painted', issued to the 97th); swords; and brass shoe-buckles. When Sir James Grant attempted to sell some of the surplus collection in 1810, he successfully disposed of all the clothing, but the buckles and knapsacks failed to attract a buyer. Along with the remainder of the collection they were placed in store at Castle Grant until 1978.

The workshops
In the centre of Prince Henry Frederick's Bastion was the workshop yard. The provision of 'sheds for carpenters, smiths and wheelwrights' shops with room for shott pounds for shott and shells' was an afterthought to the original scheme, decided upon in 1762.

The ordnance stores
The twin ordnance stores (1759-61) were for arms and military equipment. Part of the north block was adapted in the late eighteenth century as a hospital (Skinner did not provide one), and was enlarged later for the same purpose to meet higher medical standards. It is now the soldiers' mess. Part of the broad open space behind the yards of the ordnance stores was filled in 1934 by the **Seaforths' Regimental Institute** — the only completely new building in the fort. In the rampart walls either side of the open space were the **latrines** ('necessary houses'), two for officers and two for the non-commissioned officers and men. These became redundant when latrine- and ablution-blocks were added to the barracks in the nineteenth century.

The provision stores
The pair of provision stores (1760-2) housed non-military supplies. The pavilion at the south end accommodated the baker (on the first floor) above the bakery; that at the north end the brewer above his brewery. The north store was converted into detention cells in the mid nineteenth century, replacing the original 'Black Hole' beside the principal gate. The south store, gutted by fire in 1952, has since served as the sergeants' mess. Behind this store is a stone-lined **well,** one of several that were provided throughout the fort.

The ordnance stores.

The provision stores.

The chapel

The 'pritty' chapel was built in the final stages of work on the fort, an afterthought by Skinner, not part of his original scheme. The plain, handsome exterior has a polygonal chancel and a squat western tower with battlements and is flanked by rounded stair wings. Inside, a two-tiered arcade runs round three sides: the lower tier with its Roman Doric order of columns supports the gallery. A Latin inscription over the chancel arch reads: 'George III, by the grace of God King of Great Britain, France and Ireland, 1767'. Originally the three-decker pulpit, surmounted by a sounding board, stood under the middle of the chancel arch: the movement of the pulpit is the only significant change in the internal arrangement.

The east front

In the first bastioned forts the defences comprised only the rampart and a broad ditch, the latter protecting the former from distant gunfire. By improved siegecraft it became possible to bring a battery up to the outer margin of the ditch and make a breach in the rampart by close-range fire. The need to keep an attack at a safe distance led to the development of outworks such as those at Fort George.

The **principal ditch,** 300 m long and 50 m wide at the centre of the front, matches the bastions in its great scale. At either end are cross-walls called **batardeaux** which acted as dams to hold water. The ditch could be flooded at high tide by opening sluice-gates in the batardeaux (the seatings for the windlasses operating the sluices are still visible). The ditch was normally kept dry; it was always a moot point whether in time of siege a water-filled ditch was desirable. Though it was a hindrance to the enemy, it was also an obstacle to the defenders who were thus denied the cover of the ditch in moving about the outworks.

Beyond the ditch is the strongest outwork, the **ravelin.** It is completely isolated by its own ditch; the latter, with the faces of the ravelin, could be scoured by fire from the bastions. (The triangular shape of the ravelin is dictated by the need to give it complete flanking defence from the fort bastions.) The ravelin has a rampart with parapet, embrasures for eight 12-pounder guns, and a musketry firing-step on its two faces; the rear is open so that it could be commanded from the fort itself. Thus, even if the ravelin were evacuated, the defence could still contest any attempt by an enemy to

The chapel.

The ravelin bridge.

occupy it. The ravelin has its own guardhouse (now the **Visitor Centre**), and a gate leading by a tunnel to the outer defences. The bridge over the ravelin ditch had a drawbridge at the innermost span which, when raised, covered the gate.

The outer margin of the principal ditch and the ravelin ditch is closed by the **counterscarp,** a masonry wall sloping or 'battered' like the scarp. The angles have flights of steps leading into the ditches to help the concealed movements of the defenders, who could enter or leave the ravelin and the principal gate by doors at the level of the bottom of the ditch.

On top of the counterscarp is the **covered way,** 11.6 m wide. This is the outermost defensive line, so-called because it is covered from the attacking horizontal fire by a brick parapet wall. (It is not 'covered' in the sense of being roofed over.) Below the wall is an earthwork **firing-step.** Originally there was a stout wooden palisade along the front edge of the firing-step to hinder an enemy trying to jump down on to the covered way.

The covered way has two angular **places of arms,** assembly points for counter-attack. Two **lunettes** of similar shape, designed to resist penetration of the covered way, have their own little fighting platform and firing-step. Short **traverses** (with palisades and firing-steps) set across the covered way could also confine penetration, though their main function was to stop cannonballs from rolling murderously along the covered way. No cannon were mounted on the covered way; it was defended by musketeers standing on the firing-step, and by others armed with portable trench mortars. The north sea-wall of the covered way has a latrine projecting out from it. A similar latrine at the south wall was destroyed when the 1790 cutting through the glacis removed this end of the covered way.

A smoothly graded strip of ground 50 m wide, called the **glacis,** slopes from the covered way down to original ground level. As well as protecting the covered way, this earthwork helps to shield the fort rampart and ravelin from shelling. Two **cuttings** through the glacis allow rapid egress. The southern cutting carried the roads from Inverness and Nairn and the military road from Blairgowrie into the fort (this is the approach by which visitors now enter the fort). In about 1790 a third cutting was made through the glacis south of the ditch for civilian traffic to and from the ferry. This cutting accidentally helped to preserve the fort, for when the south sallyport was later

widened as the main entry, the original tortuous approach through the east front with its bridges and vaulted gates was by-passed and left intact.

Lastly, a zone, 640 m deep, was cleared right across the peninsula to remove obstructions so that the gunners on the bastion salients had an open view of targets up to 800 m away — a zone of fire which could take in the most distant works of a regular siege.

An attack on the east front could only succeed if supported by heavy artillery, advanced by stages under cover of siege earthworks. The progress of even the best-conducted operation would have been slow and painful. Their approach could be opposed by fire from guns in the bastion salients and the faces of the ravelin, and by counter-attack from the covered way and the two sallyports. The fort presented a further hazard: not only was it

The south batardeau, or cross wall.

Inset: A traverse with lunette beyond.

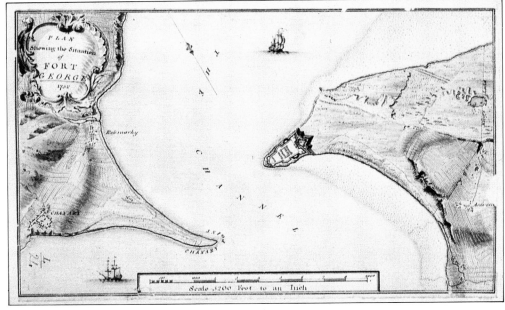

Plan of Fort George in 1752 highlighting its strategic position on a promontory projecting into the Moray Firth. When conceived, the fort's main threat was from a landward invasion and the need for the fortress to be capable of being supplied from the sea was paramount in the mind of the Fort's designer.

impossible to cut siege trenches into the shingle of the peninsula without special shoring, but the shingle would also break into dangerous flying splinters under fire. Penetration of the covered way was obstructed by the traverses and lunettes placed in it. If they were taken, the defence could withdraw to the ravelin. If that in turn were lost, the defence could be prolonged from the bastions and curtains until one of them was breached at point-blank range by batteries emplaced on the crest of the glacis. Only then could the final assault be made with any confidence of success.

No attempt has ever been made, not by Jacobite, by Frenchman or any other. Not a single shot has been fired in anger from the ramparts. General Skinner's defences on the east front have never been altered, and nowhere else in Britain can so complete a view be obtained of the defensive system of an eighteenth-century artillery fort.

Books

No full study of Fort George has been published (although there are two articles on the fort in *Country Life*, for 12 and 19 August 1976) and there is no detailed overall treatment of its background. Most of the facts in this guide-book are taken from manuscripts and plans in the National Library of Scotland, the Public Record Office, the British Museum and elsewhere. The fort and its background are included by Stewart Cruden in the last chapter of *The Scottish Castle* (1981) but the account is meant as no more than a summary postscript to the book's theme. John Fleming in *Robert Adam and His Circle* (1962) mentions the connection of the Adam family with the fort. Fragments of the background are dealt with in several places: C H Firth, *Scotland and the Protectorate* (1899) on the Cromwellian fortifications; the *Stirlingshire* Inventory of the Royal Commission on the Ancient and Historical Monuments of Scotland (1963) on Inversnaid, one of the 1717 barracks; J B Salmond on *Wade in Scotland* (1934); W D Simpson, *Proceedings of the Society of Antiquaries of Scotland* 61 (1926-27), 48-103 on Corgarff Castle, one of the 1748 barracks; G P Stell, *Ruthven Barracks* (SDD guide leaflet, 1983).

Friends of Scottish Monuments

Membership of the 'Friends' organisation gives you free admission to all the historic sites cared for by Historic Buildings and Monuments Directorate throughout Scotland, plus the satisfaction of registering your personal commitment to the preservation of our national heritage.
You will also get entry concessions to English and Welsh properties, and a regular newsletter keeping you up to date with historical and archaeological developments in Scotland.
As a 'Friend' you'll enjoy more of the past in the future.
Full details are available at any staffed monument or by post from Historic Buildings and Monuments, SDD, PO Box 157, Edinburgh.

Printed in Scotland for HMSO by (42080)
Dd 287125/HF4726 C130 7/88